## What's Awake?

# Raccoons

## Patricia Whitehouse

Heinemann Library

Chicago, Illinois

Customer Service  888-454-2279
Visit our website at www.heinemannlibrary.com

Designed by Sue Emerson, Heinemann Library
Printed and bound in the United States by Lake Book Manufacturing, Inc.

07 06 05 04 03
10 9 8 7 6 5 4 3 2 1

**Library of Congress Cataloging-in-Publication Data**
Whitehouse, Patricia, 1958-
    Raccoons / Patricia Whitehouse.
        p. cm. — (What's awake)
Includes index.
Summary: A basic introduction to raccoons, including their habitat, diet, and physical features
    ISBN: 1-58810-882-1 (HC), 1-40340-628-6 (Pbk.)
    1.  Raccoons—Juvenile literature. [1. raccoons.]  I. Title.
    QL737.C26 W48 2002
    599.76'32—dc21

                                    2001006396

**Acknowledgments**
The author and publishers are grateful to the following for permission to reproduce copyright material:
p. 4 Steve Strickland/Visuals Unlimited; p. 5 Joe McDonald/Visuals Unlimited; pp. 6, 9, 22 Barbara Gerlach/Visuals Unlimited; pp. 7, 12 Maslowski/Visuals Unlimited; p. 8L Kim Fennema/Visuals Unlimited; p. 8R Ken Lucas/Visuals Unlimited; p. 10 Rob Simpson/Visuals Unlimited; p. 11 John Daniels/Ardea; p. 13 Norbert Rosing/Animals Animals; pp. 14, 17 Dwight Kuhn; p. 15 Steve Maslowski/Photo Researchers, Inc.; p. 16 G. VandeLeest/Visuals Unlimited; p. 18 Mary Clay/Ardea; pp. 19, 20 Rob & Ann Simpson/Visuals Unlimited; p. 21 C. C. Lockwood/DRK Photo

Cover photograph by C. K. Lorenz/Photo Researchers, Inc.

Every effort has been made to contact copyright holders of any material reproduced in this book.
Any omissions will be rectified in subsequent printings if notice is given to the publisher.

Special thanks to our advisory panel for their help in the preparation of this book:

Eileen Day, Preschool Teacher
Chicago, IL

Ellen Dolmetsch,
Library Media Specialist
Wilmington, DE

Kathleen Gilbert,
Teacher
Round Rock, TX

Sandra Gilbert,
Library Media Specialist
Houston, TX

Angela Leeper,
Educational Consultant
North Carolina Department
of Public Instruction
Raleigh, NC

Pam McDonald, Reading Teacher
Winter Springs, FL

Melinda Murphy,
Library Media Specialist
Houston, TX

The publisher would also like to thank Dr. Dennis Radabaugh, Professor of Zoology at Ohio Wesleyan University in Delaware, Ohio, for his help in reviewing the contents of this book.

Some words are shown in bold, **like this.**
You can find them in the picture glossary on page 23.

# Contents

# What's Awake?

Some animals are awake when you go to sleep.

Animals that stay awake at night are **nocturnal**.

Raccoons are awake at night.

# What Are Raccoons?

Raccoons are **mammals**.

Mammals have **fur**.

Mammals live with their babies.

They make milk for the babies.

# What Do Raccoons Look Like?

raccoon

cat

Raccoons look like cats.

They have gray and black **fur**.

fur

rings

The black fur around their eyes looks like a **mask**.

They have black rings on their tails.

# Where Do Raccoons Live?

Raccoons' homes are called **dens**.

In the wild, they live in **hollow** trees.

In the city, raccoons live in trees or near houses.

# What Do Raccoons Do at Night?

Raccoons wake up after dark.

They look for food.

They may cross roads to look
for food.

# What Do Raccoons Eat?

In the wild, raccoons eat frogs.

They eat plants and fish, too.

In the city, raccoons eat food from garbage cans.

They also eat food people leave out for their pets.

# What Do Raccoons Sound Like?

Raccoons can growl or bark.

Raccoons scream if they are afraid.

# How Are Raccoons Special?

Raccoons have **paws** that look like hands.

They use their paws to hold food.

Raccoons are very good climbers.

They are good swimmers, too.

# Where Do Raccoons Go during the Day?

In the morning, raccoons find a safe place.

They go to sleep.

Sometimes raccoons sleep in strange places.

These raccoons are in a **chimney**.

# Raccoon Map

fur

mask

paw

tail

# Picture Glossary

 **chimney**
page 21

 **mammal**
pages 6, 7

 **den**
page 10

 **mask**
page 9

 **fur**
pages 6, 8, 9

 **nocturnal**
page 4

 **hollow**
page 10

 **paws**
page 18

23

# Note to Parents and Teachers

Reading for information is an important part of a child's literacy development. Learning begins with a question about something. Help children think of themselves as investigators and researchers by encouraging their questions about the world around them. In this book, the animal is identified as a mammal. A mammal by definition is one that is covered with hair or fur and that feeds its young with milk from its body. The symbol for mammal in the picture glossary is of a dog nursing its babies. Point out the fact that, although the photograph for mammal shows a dog, many other animals are mammals—including humans.

 **CAUTION:** Remind children that it is not a good idea to handle wild animals. Children should wash their hands with soap and water after they touch any animal.

# Index

24